PRAGUE CASTLE

BONECHI & NEPALA

Distributed by:

Nepala, spol. s.r.o., Horňátecká 1772/19 - 182 00 PRAHA 8
tel.: +420 28468 6704 fax: +420 28468 6606
mobil: +420 775 368449 / +420 602 368449
e-mail: nepala@bonechi.cz - internet: www.bonechi.cz

Project and design: *Casa Editrice Bonechi*
Editorial direction: *Monica Bonechi*
Graphic design: *Monica Bonechi*
Layout, cover and graphics: *Elena Nannucci*
Texts: *Patrizia Fabbri*
Translation: *Eve Leckey*
Illustration pages 4-5: *Stefano Benini* Illustrations on cover and p. 46: *Sauro Giampaia*

© Copyright by Casa Editrice Bonechi, Via Cairoli 18/b, Florence - Italy
E-mail: bonechi@bonechi.it

Printed in Italy by *Centro Stampa Editoriale Bonechi* - Sesto Fiorentino.

The photographs in this publication belong to the archive of *Casa Editrice Bonechi* and were taken by
Marco Bonechi, Andrea Pistolesi.

Additional contributions by:
© *Picture Library of the Prague Castle*: photos on pages 22, 23, 45, 48, 49.

The photographs on page 62 were kindly provided by the *National Gallery in Prague.*

The publisher wishes to thank *Dr. František Kadlec*, Director of the Department of Tourism
for his invaluable assistance in revising the texts.

The publisher apologises for any omissions and is willing to make amends with the formal recognition
of the author of any photo subsequently identified.

ISBN-10 88-476-2076-7
ISBN-13 978-88-476-2076-6

Internet: www.bonechi.com

INTRODUCTION

No longer encumbered by its original function as a purely defensive stronghold, today Prague Castle is more like a small town presenting a harmonious appearance, as the various separate components have been quite elegantly unified. The residence of the dukes of Bohemia was situated on this hill as early as the 980s when prince Bořivoj founded the first royal palace here. According to legend, princess Libuše originally foresaw its foundation in a prophetic vision and predicted that a rich and powerful city would arise on this green slope on the river Vltava. It is also said that an ancient Slav place of worship was located here. In any case, St Mary's Church was built here at the end of the 9th century and in about 920 duke Vratislav I also built the church dedicated to St George and consecrated in 925. Not long after, the Rotunda of St Vitus was built by Wenceslas, who would subsequently be assassinated and then too join the glorious ranks of the saints. In the 10th century the Castle was more or less exactly the same size as that of today and an early wooden fortification probably also existed. Frequently besieged and destroyed and just as frequently rebuilt and fortified, the Castle experienced a long period of energetic development from the 12th century when the Přemyslid princes took up residence there. Under Přemysl Otakar I, Wenceslas I and Přemysl Otakar II, despite long periods of war and threats of invasion, the Castle buildings increased and included the Royal Palace, the Romanesque part of which was begun by Soběslav I in the first half of the 12th century; enlarged and modernised in 1252 by the future Otakar II, it was entirely destroyed by a storm in 1280. Under Wenceslas II and his son Wenceslas III, repair and restoration work was only slowly undertaken. An unfortunate period followed under John of Luxembourg and the Castle was neglected, but during the mid 14th century, his son, Charles IV, who had been educated at the court of France, built a new Royal Palace and Cathedral worthy of the newly flourishing city, thus bringing a sophisticated and previously unknown splendour to the Castle. In turn his son, Wenceslas

IV, continued and extended his father's achievements. A series of rulers followed who were more interested in wars than in improving the capital of the kingdom until finally Vladislav II Jagellonsky turned his attention to the Castle at the start of the 16th century. He was responsible for the new fortifications but also for a series of new buildings and plans. With the arrival of Ferdinand I, a member of the Hapsburg family (1526-1564), it was decided that the Castle required a new look and character, more suited to the requirements of an important court: gardens were created, buildings were enlarged and its magnificence increased. The devastating fire of 1541 made radical rebuilding urgent and also facilitated the work of improvement and development instigated by first Maximilian II and then Rudolph II (an art lover and enthusiast of the sciences, who enriched the Castle with both his numerous collections and his illustrious scholarly guests, such as Tycho de Brahe and Kepler. In the early 17th century under Ferdinand II the Baroque was splendidly introduced to the Castle and its gardens. The style continued to develop under Ferdinand III, Leopold I (who laid the first stone of the Cathedral's Baroque completion in 1673) and Charles VI. Finally, in the mid 18th century, Maria Theresa of Austria commissioned the court architect, Nicola Pacassi, to plan and carry out the definitive appearance and arrangement of the general structure. The Castle then fell into a kind of oblivion, only interrupted by sporadic and sumptuous coronation ceremonies. Impoverished by expropriations and damaged by extensive military use of its buildings, it came to life once more under Ferdinand V who chose it as his personal residence, and its role was once again reasserted in the 20th century when the Republic came into being. The Castle was chosen as the natural residence for the President and was restored and adapted for its new purpose by Josip Plečnik. More recently Vaclav Havel initiated the restoration of many rooms and areas that had for long been neglected and inaccessible; returned once more to their original splendour, these are now open to the public.

PRAGUE CASTLE

Chapel of the Holy Cross

St George and the dragon

*The ancient passage linking the **Cathedral** to the Royal Palace*

Cathedral of St Vitus
*with the imposing **royal mausoleum**, created by the Hapsburgs, with sculptural figures of Ferdinand I and Anna Jagellonsky and their son, Maximilian II.*

ROYAL GARDENS

North Gate

RIDING SCHOOL GARDENS

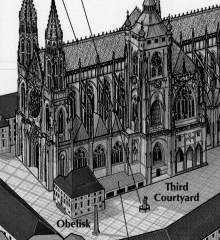

THE GARDEN ON THE BASTION

Matthias' Gate

First Courtyard

Second Courtyard

NORTH WING

WEST WING

Third Courtyard

Obelisk

SOUTH WING

GARDENS

SOUTH

Hradčanské náměstí
the large square in front of the Castle

Giants' Gate

PARADISE GARDEN

Archaeological excavations
*that have brought to light the **pre-romanesque** Rotunda of St Vitus*

The Summer Palace of Queen Anne

St George's
Basilica

Golden Lane

**ROYAL
GARDENS**

East Gate

Black Tower

St George's Monastery

Lobkovicz Palace

National Gallery
in Prague

St George's Square

**SOUTH
GARDENS**

**SOUTH
GARDENS**

**The Old Castle
Stairway,**
*a romantic and almost
legendary part of
Prague, celebrated in
popular songs, which
leads down into the
city from the East Gate.*

Ludvík Wing

GARDEN ON THE RAMPARTS

The ancient **Royal Palace**

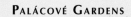

PALÁCOVÉ GARDENS

*South of the Castle below what was
once an impressive system of defensive
ramparts and where there was parkland
and vineyards in the 16th century, the
elegant* **"Palace Gardens"** *have recently
been splendidly restored.*

**HARTIG
GARDEN**

WELCOME TO THE CASTLE:

THE ENTRANCES

From Hradčanské náměstí

From the East Gate

From the North Gate

Historically the main entrance to the Castle is on the west side, approached from the extensive and panoramic *Hradčanské náměstí*, the "Square of the Hradčanské District" – the Castle District. The entire city can be seen from here, lying below this historic group of buildings.

This ancient entrance is now surrounded by more recent buildings. It stands beneath the sombre Black Tower and is reached from a panoramic stairway.

In the past this Renaissance entrance was not considered very important as it was not a ceremonial entrance. Today instead it is much used by tourists as there are convenient car parks nearby.

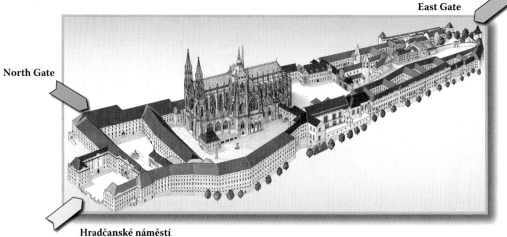

East Gate

North Gate

Hradčanské náměstí

Under the stern gaze of the statue of Masaryk and accompanied by the romantic music of street musicians, visitors arrive at the Castle passing the elegant flight of steps and buildings that enhance Hradčany Square.

Above, a view of the Archbishop's Palace, situated in the Square.

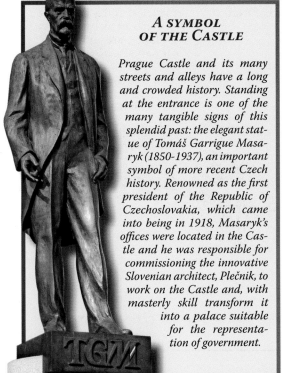

A SYMBOL OF THE CASTLE

Prague Castle and its many streets and alleys have a long and crowded history. Standing at the entrance is one of the many tangible signs of this splendid past: the elegant statue of Tomáš Garrigue Masaryk (1850-1937), an important symbol of more recent Czech history. Renowned as the first president of the Republic of Czechoslovakia, which came into being in 1918, Masaryk's offices were located in the Castle and he was responsible for commissioning the innovative Slovenian architect, Plečnik, to work on the Castle and, with masterly skill transform it into a palace suitable for the representation of government.

Hradčanské náměstí

Our tour to visit this vast and complex civic monument begins from the large square in front of the Castle, from where we enter the majestic **Giants' Gate**. It is worth pausing first however, to observe the dignified buildings that surround the square, all of which are of great architectural interest, in particular the elegant **Archbishop's Palace**. Originally a Renaissance building, it was first altered in the second half of the 16th century, extended about 1600 and then modified in the new Baroque style during the second half of the 17th century. The façade was given its present rococo appearance in the second half of the 18th century by J. J. Wirch, providing a more suitable frame for the splendid main entrance designed during the late 17th century by J. B. Mathey.

GIANTS' GATE

Clearly Hapsburg in style, the name of the gate is derived from the *gigantic figures* which dominate the pillars at the entrance, designed by I. Platzer the Elder and made between 1770 and 1771. All along the railings on either side of the gate, are more statues portraying cherubs, an eagle, (a symbol of the Hapsburg rulers), and a lion (animal symbolizing the kingdom of Bohemia), forming a varied series of contemporary works, also by Ignác Platzer. The figures seen here today are copies however, as the originals, made of sandstone that is badly affected by climatic conditions, were removed and replaced at the beginning of the 20th century.

First Courtyard

The Castle Gate leads into the Ceremonial Courtyard (or First Courtyard). This is located where once there was a deep ravine dividing the district of Hradčany from the older buildings of the Castle, and only crossed by bridges. This court was also built during the Hapsburg period (1763-1771) when Maria Theresa of Austria instructed the court architect Nicola Picassi, assisted by the master builder A. Lurago, to design this great square where the pre-existing gully had been filled in. To give the square an elegant appearance the architect created three fine buildings in the Viennese style, forming a majestic U shape. Thus the concept of the defensive fortress was clearly abandoned and the appearance of the Castle began to evolve into that of an airy imperial residence. This continued with the construction of the New Palace which would later be extended with the addition of the buildings that surround the Second Courtyard. The halls, apartments and rooms of the **North** and **South Wings** are still used for state visits, while the **West Wing** is generally used for official receptions and events.

Below, together with the official corps (left), the mighty stone colossi guard the elaborate Giants' Gate, named after them.

Above, the Giants' Gate precedes Matthias Gate, made of sandstone, which originally stood alone like a triumphal arch.

MATTHIAS' GATE

Preceded by two lofty flag staffs 25 metres high, originally made from the trunk of a single fir tree from Moravia, wedged between the buildings of the West Wing the 17th-century Matthias' Gate leads to the Second Courtyard. Like a solitary triumphal arch, it was erected by Matthias II in 1614 (and is therefore much earlier than the buildings that surround it) in early baroque style though with Rudolphesque influences, it was probably the work of the court architect, Giovanni Mario Filippi, though it has also been suggested that the design was by Scamozzi. It is clearly a commemorative structure: engraved at the top are the titles and heraldic emblem of Emperor Matthias, while below, beneath the cornice, are the numerous coats of arms of the countries in his domain. Access to the various rooms of the splendid West Wing is from here, via the two stairways that lead out of the entrance way.

THE CHANGING OF THE GUARD

For centuries a small group of guards has protected the safety of the castle. Though today they wear elegant modern uniforms newly designed in 1989 by Theodor Pištěk, life was rather more difficult in the past in particular in the 18th century when, only paid with free lodging and wood for their fires for warmth, they were reduced to only 24 men armed with barely three bullets each. The institution of the castle guards survived, however, and even now every day on the hour from 5 in the morning until 11 pm the changing of the guard is performed in front of the gates. The most spectacular of these ceremonies however, takes place at midday under the eyes of an admiring public, complete with brass fanfares and the exchange of flags.

West Wing

Still used today for purely ceremonial functions, the West Wing is approached from two *stairways* at the Matthias' Gate: the monumental stair on the right was made at the time of Maria Theresa by Nicola Pacassi, replacing a less grandiose one built by Rudolph II to provide access to his private apartments. Previously in fact, some separate and independent buildings existed in this area and were later incorporated into the new Hapsburg structure, aptly named the New Palace. Housing a stupendous series of bright and sophisticated salons, this wing lies between the First and Second Courtyards and at the southern end is the sumptuous **Throne Room**, where the president of the Republic now receives guests of the State. Also here is the grand **Hapsburg Salon**, its splendid 18th-century decoration still intact and enhanced by a gallery of portraits of relations of the Empress Maria Theresa. Continuing along the West Wing towards the north the austere but

Left, the Hall of Columns, a masterpiece in the West Wing. Above, view from the splendid Gallery extending between the First and Second Courtyard.

light **Hall of Columns** is reached, made between 1927 and 1931 by Josip Plečnik with a new stair added in 1975. Access to one of the most important areas of the presidential quarters in the Castle is from here.

The Garden on the Bastion

Outside the West Wing, beyond a small courtyard in the North Wing of the First Courtyard, in 1930 Josip Plečnik created an attractive garden which is approached from a circular stair and has a sophisticated geometrical formation composed of flowerbeds, bushes and paths. A long balcony overlooks the Deer Moat. The name of the Gardens is derived from the remains of a rampart dating from the time of the Přemyslid, which in the past was used as a platform for defensive cannon.

Second Courtyard

Older than the preceding court (its construction began in the 15th century), and also built over a pre-existing moat that enclosed and protected the Romanesque city walls, the Second Courtyard was surrounded by buildings in different styles, from different periods and with different purposes, often also quite separate and independent from each other. It was only with the 18th-century project of Pacassi that the courtyard assumed a harmonious and unified aspect. Newly paved during the 1970s, in the centre of the court stands an elegant baroque **fountain** designed with a mythological theme by Francesco Torre in 1686 and decorated by the sculptor Jeronym Kohl. Nearby is an old **well**, for long a fundamental source for supplying water, which was decorated in the 18th century with an unusual net-like design in wrought iron to crown it, reminiscent of a birdcage. In the past, close by and joined to the West Wing, was the oldest Castle church, the renowned St Mary's church which dated from as early as the 9th century.

North Gate

The North Gate lies in the shadow of the Cathedral towers and is reached from the Powder Bridge spanning the Deer Moat. It is flanked by the stables built by Rudolph II for the Spanish horses and provides an entrance towards the gardens of Renaissance origin, although the façade towards the gardens was in fact designed by Nicola Pacassi.

Opposite page, the Second Courtyard with the fountain and well; below, the modern canopy that protects the entrance to the Chancellery of the President of the Republic.

North Wing

The Second Courtyard is framed by various buildings, including the North Wing with an entrance way, the North Gate, leading out of the castle complex to the Powder Bridge over the Deer Moat and generally much more frequented now than in the past. Situated here are the vast **Renaissance Stables**, built in the late 16th century by Rudolph II to provide a suitable home for his magnificent Spanish horses. However, located on the upper floors are two of the Castle's finest gems: the Spanish Hall and the **Gallery of Rudolph II**. An enthusiastic and eclectic collector, principally of works of art

and especially paintings, Emperor Rudolph created a vast and rare collection and commissioned G. Gargiolli to design the most suitable setting possible for them in the stable block; the splendid *Rudolph Gallery* was enhanced with fine bas reliefs in the 19th century. As time passed, however, the prestigious imperial collection seemed destined to be dismantled: on several occasions many works were transferred to Vienna, while others were sold and yet more were pillaged during the all-too-frequent wars and battles (in particular during the war against Sweden). However, opened in 1965 in the old stable building, today's gallery

is still based on the original nucleus of precisely the imperial collections of Rudolph and can boast masterpieces by Paolo Veronese, Rubens, Titian and Tintoretto, flanked by more recent paintings from the 18th, 19th and 20th centuries by artists of Prague. Just as interesting, and designed by G. M. Filippi, is the enormous **Spanish Hall**, occupying two floors of the North Wing and originally built between 1602 and 1606, but refurbished several times in the 18th and 19th centuries giving it the clearly baroque appearance remaining today. Not even the pillars that supported the roof of the original structure have survived, but were eliminated during 18th-century rebuilding undertaken by I. Dientzenhofer and A. Lurago who replaced them with an innovative system of trusses and bracing of the vaults. The last alterations made during the late 19th century were intended as a setting for a historical event that never took place – the coronation ceremony of Francis Joseph as sovereign of the Czech nation. Also furnished to house the collections of the emperor, the Spanish Hall has gradually assumed a purely formal role instead, hosting court celebrations and memorable balls.

Magnificent views of the splendid Spanish Hall, without doubt one of the most important in the entire Castle and, below, the Gallery of Rudolph II, nearby.

South Wing

A central wing which incorporates the ancient **Bishop's Tower** (equipped by Rudolph II with an excellent astronomical observatory) and which also housed some of his artistic collections in the past, leads south to the remains of the equally old **White Tower**. Some 30 metres high, this constitutes another impressive element of the massive Romanesque fortifications which once stood here and are still partially visible in the existing buildings. As early as the 12th century this grim tower was used as a fearsome prison and in the course of centuries hosted various illustrious prisoners including king Wenceslas IV. Subsequently, during the second half of the 18th century, the reliable Pacassi reduced its height by removing the top storey at the time of rebuilding the entire South Wing which had until then been completely fragmentary and lacking in any coherence. Thus, closing the Second Courtyard, the fourth wing came into being in perfect harmony with those already existing. The buildings that form this wing are used for formal and ceremonial functions today and the president's apartments and offices are located here, between the Central and the South Wings.

CHAPEL OF THE HOLY CROSS

In the south-east area of the Second Courtyard is the simple and elegant Chapel of the Holy Cross, built by A. Lurago between 1758 and 1763 according to a design by Nicola Pacassi. However, all that remains of that period are the high altar made by Ignác Platzer and a *Crucifix* painted by S. Balko. All the rest of the building dates from the 19th century restoration, resulting from the need to adapt the building to its role as a private chapel for the emperor.

The splendid and opulent interior of the Chapel of the Holy Cross.

Third Courtyard

An entrance set into the Central wing, where robust remains of the Romanesque fortifications can still be seen, leads into the heart of the Castle, the large third courtyard, originally on two levels that were merged during the 20th century by the spectacular paving in granite by Plečnik. Modern and old features mingle harmoniously in this area, with the Cathedral towering above. Archaeological excavations have for long investigated the historical and architectural history of the original nucleus of the Castle here. The **Old Provost's House**, built on the site of the Romanesque Bishop's palace of which an original window survives, is flanked by a many modern and linear granite **monoliths**.

SAINT GEORGE AND THE DRAGON

Patron of knights and soldiers, perhaps no saint is so popularly venerated as Saint George. He is most often shown in his epic battle with the dragon, representing an intrepid image of the defender of Good, capable of opposing and defeating Evil. The extent of his cult and popularity is evident in the numerous churches dedicated to him. Prague Castle is also among these and has consecrated a church and monastery to him as well as a sculptural monument located beside the majestic Cathedral. However, the figure that is seen in the Third Courtyard today is only a copy of the 14th-century bronze equestrian group portraying the saint as he vanquishes the dragon. The original is now housed in the old Royal Palace.

Left, the Old Provost's House, showing the archaeological site alongside where findings would seem to suggest the existence of a necropolis.

A MODERN OBELISK

Tall and slender, almost 18 metres in height, made of marble from Mrákotín, the evocative Monolith in the Third Courtyard was a monument that Plečnik strongly desired should be raised in memory of the victims of the First World War on the occasion of an important celebration – the 10th anniversary of the birth of the first Republic of Czechoslovakia.

Cathedral of St Vitus

*T*he history of Prague Cathedral, the true spiritual centre of the entire country, is lengthy and complex. In 925, where this impressive monument now stands, St Wenceslas built the small circular Romanesque structure of St Vitus, his future burial place, flanked not long afterwards by the bishops' residence and subsequently replaced in 1060 by a new basilica with three naves and two choirs. It was not until 1344 that Charles IV commissioned the French architect, Mathieu d'Arras, to build a new Gothic cathedral for the rapidly growing city, which had recently become an archbishopric – a cathedral that would be worthy of housing the body of such a great sovereign as St Wenceslas, the country's patron. The foundation stone was laid on 21 November of that year and the great French cathedrals provided the model for the construction. When Mathieu d'Arras died the work was continued, under the guidance and direct control of Charles IV, by the Swabian architect and sculptor, Petr Parléř, one of the fathers of European Gothic, until his death in 1399. His sons, Jan and Wenceslas, took over but work was interrupted in the 1420s by the Hussite wars. At the time, most of the bell tower had been built but not even half of the building was completed, and the choir was closed with a wall forming a kind of temporary façade so that religious services could be held. The ambulatory and a first Renaissance dome were built in the second half of the 16th century. Thus the Cathedral remained unfinished, with a truncated appearance – the nave barely begun beyond the transept. A series of disastrous events then followed: in 1541 there was a dreadful fire, in 1620 it was pillaged by the Calvinists, a century later it was severely attacked and damaged by the Prussians, and in 1760 lightning struck causing another fire as well as destroying the only existing tower at the time. The work of building the west nave did not then begin until 1872 when Joseph Mocker's project continued the work in complete harmony with the monumental style already existing. When Mocker died, Kamil Hilbert took over in 1899 and in 1929, one thousand years after the death of St Wenceslas, the Cathedral, with its imperious stature and interwoven buttresses so characteristic of the most perfect Gothic architecture, could finally be said to be finished.

WEST FAÇADE

Framed by two lofty *twin towers* ending in soaring spires (82 metres high, compared to the 99,6 of the south tower), the 20th-century façade has three sections formed by spires, statues and elegant neo-Gothic decorative elements, including the traditional gargoyles, and is dominated by the large rose window designed between 1925 and 1927 by František Kysela. Lower down, three elaborate but elegant entrances with bas-reliefs portraying scenes from the life of St Wenceslas (on the left) and St Adalbert (on the right) and events during the construction of the Cathedral (in the centre), provide access to the well-lit nave.

*The splendid main façade of the Cathedral of St Vitus,
with details of the central doorway and some of the bas-reliefs that decorate it.*

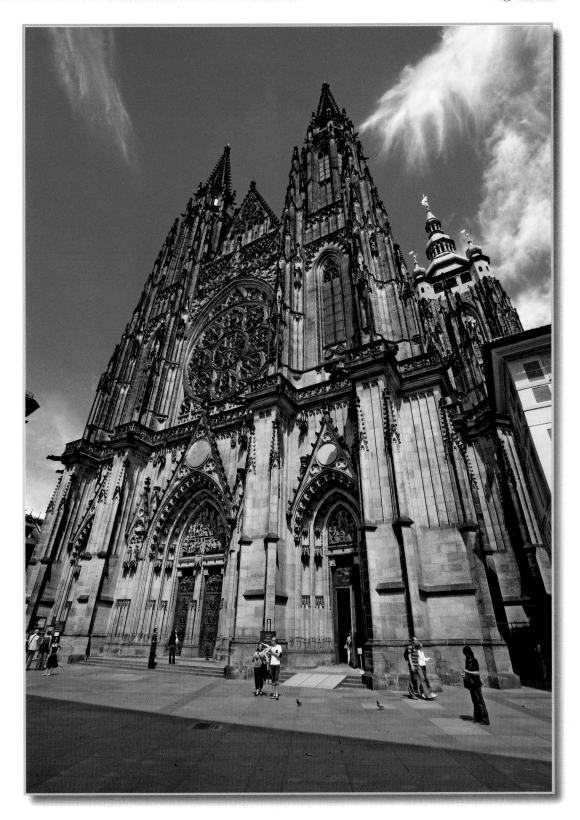

SOUTH FAÇADE

This side is almost considered to be the main entrance to the great Cathedral and indeed for centuries it was the only one to provide access. The 14th century south façade is embellished with the magnificent **Golden Door**, crowned by a mosaic of the *Universal Judgement*, made about 1370. The three arches of the entrance lead to the renowned and beautifully decorated stone vestibule. On the right, a spiral staircase enclosed by a splendid stone shell, artistically engraved, leads to the external triforium. On the left, and even more impressive, is the *south tower*, raised to a height of more than 50 metres by Petr Parléř but only finished two centuries later with the elegant gilded grating, the clock with two faces, the 16-17th century bells (the largest is nicknamed Sigismund), and ending in a dome redesigned by Nicola Pacassi in baroque style.

Right and below, views of the south façade of the Cathedral, showing the impressive tower crowned by a baroque cupola designed by Pacassi.

Left, the splendid apse, decorated with spires and pinnacles, is illuminated by stained glass windows and surrounded by chapels in the French Gothic style.

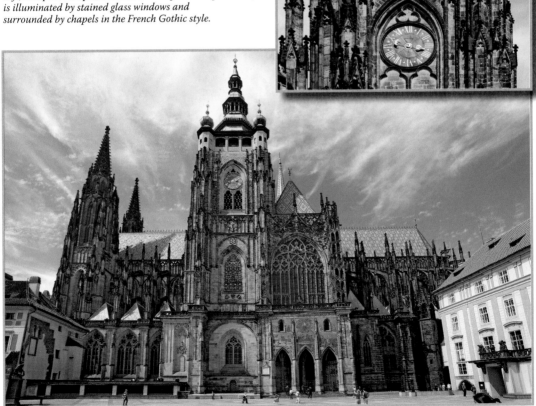

Above, the Gothic plaque to the left of the Golden Door, recording the building of the Cathedral; below, Gothic ribbing in the roofing of the vestibule.

THE UNIVERSAL JUDGEMENT

A true masterpiece of 14th century Gothic, this elaborate mosaic masterpiece is centred around the figure of Christ who stands above man in judgment and probably follows a design by Venetian masters. Beneath are six patron saints of Bohemia in the act of praying and worshipping. Further below, on either side of the pointed arch and also in the act of praying, are the figures of Charles IV and his fourth wife, Elizabeth of Pomerania. Also to the sides are the apostles and two scenes which most probably had a great emotional effect, as well as having a didactic function – Damnation and Resurrection.

Opposite page, the mosaic of the Universal Judgement.
This page, above, the modern mosaic portraying
Adam and Eve in the south vestibule.

Cathedral of St Vitus

THE INTERIOR

Some 124 metres long, just over 33 high, 60 metres at the widest point of the transept, with two lower naves flanking the central one, the interior of St Vitus' Cathedral is austere, unadorned and harmonious. Light filters through the large stained glass windows and below these, with a height of about 14 metres, runs an elegant and original ambulatory, known as the **internal triforium or arcade**, decorated with a magnificent gallery of sculptures. Below is a long sequence of **chapels**, some of which are antique and were designed by Mathieu d'Arras and Petr Parléř, some of which are more recent. Overhead is the spectacular, uninterrupted interlacing of the meshed pattern in the **vaults**, a genuine innovation in 14th century Europe and once more created by the genius of Petr Parléř. On the west side is the kaleidoscopic colour effect of the **stained glass window**; 27,000 pieces of coloured glass form scenes from the *Creation*. Occupying the centre of the nave is the *burial place of St Adalbert*, for whom a chapel was first built on the exterior of the provisional west façade of the unfinished Cathedral, though this was later destroyed when building work began once more. On the east side is the transept which crosses the nave more or less at the point where building of the Cathedral was interrupted in the 15th century. Standing guard at the majestic intersection of nave and transept are eight wooden statues of the patron saints of Bohemia: Adalbert, John Nepomucene, Ludmilla, Norbert, Procopius, Sigismund, Wenceslas and Vitus.

The lofty central nave of the Cathedral, enhanced with unusual interlacing in the vault, the glowing rose window, and the brightly coloured stained glass windows in the apse.

BONU VLASTI KU CHVALE
UMĚNÍ KE CTI VĚNUJE
BANKA SLAVIE

MODERN TREASURES

Some important works of modern art are also housed in this prestigious Gothic setting, highlighting the unusual events related to this Cathedral, whose history is divided chronologically into two quite distinct parts. One example is the *wooden altar* in symbolist style (1927) with a **Crucifixion** above, dated 1899 and both made by František Bílek for the New Sacristy. Also worthy of note are the splendid and colourful stained glass windows by F. Kysela, M. Švabinský and in particular by **Alfons Mucha** (1860-1939), rightly considered to be one of the foremost Art-nouveau designers and decorators in the world.

The north part of the transept ends in a magnificent Renaissance tribune which was originally used as a monumental and temporary closure for the choir in the unfinished Cathedral (it was transferred here in 1924), now finished with an 18th-century organ. The south end is lit by a glistening neo-Gothic *stained glass window*, the panes of which represent scenes from the *Universal Judgment*, made in 1939 by Max Švabinský. Lit by three large windows of 20th-century stained glass is the grand *apse*, preceded by the impressive **royal mausoleum** made by the Hapsburgs at the end of the 16th century, where the reclining figures of Ferdinand I, his wife, Anna Jagellonsky and their son, Maximilian II are visible behind the statue of the *Risen Christ*. Made by Alexander Collin between 1570 and 1589, this grandiose marble monument is a magnificent conclusion to the **royal crypt** below. Reached from the Chapel of the Holy Cross and rebuilt in the first half of the 20th century, various members of the imperial family have been interred here, behind an elegant enclosure, since the late 16th century.

Left, the splendid modern stained glass windows created by the artistic genius of Alfons Mucha.
Below, the solemn royal mausoleum of the Hapsburgs beside the elaborate pulpit.

THE CHAPELS

There are some 19 chapels in the Cathedral, from the nave to the apse and the south tower. All are splendid and some more grandiose than others. The **Chapel of St Sigismund** is an architectural work by Petr Parléř. The **Chapel of St John the Baptist**, originally an old structure but rebuilt in the 19th century, houses the Gothic tombs of princes Bořivoj II and Boleslav II as well as the 16th-century tombs of archbishops Antonín Brusa of Mohelnice and Martin Medek. The **Chapel of the Virgin Mary** was commissioned to be built by Charles IV on the spot where the foundation stone of the Cathedral was laid, and is opposite the *tomb of St Vitus*. Among the oldest in Europe, in the **Chapel of the Holy Reliquaries** are the magnificent sepulchres of Přemysl Otakar I and Přemysl Otakar II, whose burial crown, imperial orb and sceptre have been discovered. But the most beautiful, famous and frequently visited is without doubt the **Chapel of St Wenceslas**, on the east side of the south tower, corresponding to the apse of the old Romanesque rotunda, commissioned by Charles IV and built by Petr Parléř who completed it in 1367.

*Opposite page, the **Chapel of St Sigismund** a fine architectural work by Petr Parléř, housing the remains of this Bourbon king which were sent to Prague by Charles IV. Renaissance frescoes illustrate scenes from the life of the saint. The altar is a splendidly opulent baroque piece by Ferdinand Maximiliàn Kaňka.*

*Behind the choir stalls some splendid **wood bas-reliefs** illustrate the events of the Rebellion of the Bohemian states between 1618 and 1620. In particular, the illustration of the **Flight of Frederick of Palatine from Prague** provides an excellent view over the city. The work is by the famous court cabinet maker, Gaspar Bechteler and dates from before 1630.*

*The monumental **statue of cardinal Bedřich Schwarzenberg**, archbishop of Prague (1892-1895), commissioned by his successor, cardinal Schönborn and made by J. V. Myslbek, one of the foremost representatives of sculpture at the time of the National Renaissance. It is located in front of the Pernštejn Chapel.*

The **Chapel of the Holy Reliquaries**, also known as the Saxon Chapel, contains the marl stone **sepulchres** (below) **of the sovereigns Otakar I and Otakar II** (the funerary crown, imperial orb and sceptre, one of the oldest in Europe, of the latter have been found), made in the 14th century by Petr Parléř. Interesting old frescoes have been discovered on the walls (above).

Facing towards the Chapel of the Virgin Mary, the **altar** indicating the location of the **tomb of St Vitus** has stood beneath the stained glass window of the Holy Trinity since 1840. The sandstone statue is a 19th-century work by Emanuel Max.

TOMB OF ST JOHN NEPOMUCENE

Opposite the Chapel of St John Nepomucene, enhanced by an altar containing the relics of St Adalbert and by silver busts of Sts Cyril, Methodius, Wenceslas and Adalbert, is the funerary monument of St John Nepomucene, a masterpiece of 18th-century Bohemian art.

Made of splendidly worked silver, the monument is framed by an elegant canopy donated by the Empress Maria Theresa. Dominated by the imposing figure of the saint kneeling, the tomb is the work of Josef Emanuel Fischer of Erlach (1733-1737).

The spectacular and dramatic **Royal Oratory** was built by king Vladislav Jagellonsky in 1493. Set on a background of elaborate naturalistic motifs are the coats of arms of all the countries then under the dominion of the Jagellonsky. High above are painted figures, here representing miners with long aprons, a most significant homage to the precious silver mines that were fundamental to the power of the Jagellonsky. Also of considerable interest, on a capital nearby are two figures of Adam and Eve representing one of the oldest sculptural works existing in the Cathedral (below right).

THE FACES OF THE TRIFORIUM

*Mathieu d'Arras,
the first master builder
of the Cathedral*

*Petr Parléř,
the second master builder
of the Cathedral*

*John Henry, brother of
Charles IV, duke of Carinthia
and Tyrol, margrave of Moravia*

A most famous feature of the Cathedral triforium (blind arcade) is the amazing series of busts that decorate it, beginning with the 14ᵗʰ century works of Petr Parléř and ending with the modern sculptures dating from the 19ᵗʰ century. Thus the oldest are the portraits of eleven members of Charles IV's family (the emperor, his four wives, and their children, his parents and brothers), followed by three archbishops and, most unusually for the time, the busts of five masters of the works and the two real creators of the Cathedral, Mathieu d'Arras and Petr Parléř. Leaping ahead several centuries we find the busts of individuals who were connected with the final completion of the building. The triforium is therefore almost a paradigm of the evolution of esteem for the figure of artist and architect in the public awareness and their appreciation by patrons and institutions.

*John of Luxembourg,
king of Bohemia,
father of Charles IV*

*Elizabeth of Bohemia,
mother of Charles IV*

CHARLES IV

Emperor of the Holy Roman Empire, but also king of the Romans, king of Bohemia, count of Luxembourg and margrave of Brandenburg, this son of John of Luxembourg and Elisabeth of Bohemia was christened Wenceslas on his birth on 14 May 1316 and only took the name Charles at the time of his coronation. The first wife of Charles IV, rigorously of royal blood, was Blanche of Valois, a half sister of Philippe IV of France, who gave him two daughters – Margaret and Catherine. The second was Anne, daughter of Rudolph II of the Palatinate; the third, Anne of Schweidnitz, was the mother of Wenceslas. The fourth was Elizabeth of Pomerania who he married in 1363 and who was mother to Anne, Sigmund – the future German emperor, king of Bohemia and Hungary, and margrave of Brandenburg – John and Margaret. Certainly a numerous and complicated family, but one that not only supported him when emperor but still accompany him in his eternal and monumental resting place.

*Charles IV, king of Bohemia
and Emperor of the Holy Roman Empire*

*Blanche
de Valois,
first wife of
Charles IV*

*Anne, daughter of
Rudolph II of the
Palatinate, second wife of
Charles IV*

*Anne of Schweidnitz,
third wife of
Charles IV*

*Wenceslas IV,
son of
Charles IV
and his third
wife, Anne of
Schweidnitz*

*Elizabeth of Pomerania,
fourth wife of
Charles IV*

A sombre gateway, preceded by an Imperial 'lion rampant', leads from the archaeological site of the rotunda to the tombs of the royal crypt. Inside the cover of this book is a complete reconstruction of the crypt with detailed identification of the various tombs.

THE ROTUNDA

Archaeological excavations carried out below the Cathedral of St Vitus today have brought to light the interesting and highly

important remains of what was the ancient **pre-Romanesque rotunda of St Vitus** and the early **Romanesque basilica** with its original altar. The discovery is of great historic importance and also provides an extremely evocative access to the neighbouring **royal crypt** where lie the bodies of Charles IV, flanked by his four wives, Wenceslas IV with his wife Joanna of Bavaria, Ladislaus Posthumus and Jiří of Poděbrady. Other members of the imperial family buried here include Emperor Rudolph II, in a rare 17th-century coffin made from tin.

*Cathedral Treasury.
St Adalbert
reliquary*

*Cathedral Treasury.
Chalice made of
crystal, gilded silver
and precious gems.*

*Cathedral Treasury.
Silver reliquary of St Vitus, one
of six commissioned by king
Vladislav Jagellonsky for the
Cathedral (late 15th century).*

*Crown Jewels.
The imperial orb*

*Cathedral Treasury.
St Wenceslas reliquary*

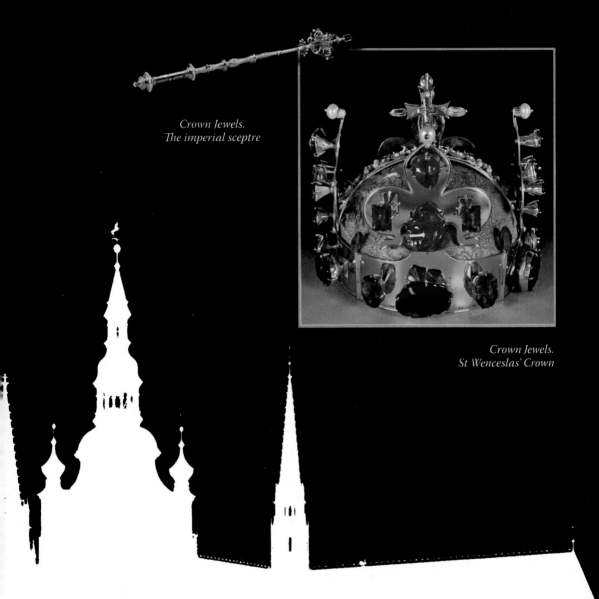

*Crown Jewels.
The imperial sceptre*

*Crown Jewels.
St Wenceslas' Crown*

THE CATHEDRAL TREASURY
AND THE CROWN JEWELS

The Cathedral of St Vitus houses and preserves priceless antique treasures of gold and silverwork. Some of these belong to the **Cathedral Treasury**, precious liturgical items dated from the 6th to 20th centuries housed alongside the **New Sacristy** on the north side of the Cathedral. Also located here is the **Old Sacristy**, formerly the Chapel of St Michael, crowned by a vault with an amazing network of ribbing that creates an original hanging keystone. Equally splendid are the **Crown Jewels**, housed in the **Crown Room** above St Wenceslas Chapel, reached from a stairway and protected by a door closed with seven locks. All the jewels are of immense value, including *St Wenceslas sword*, the *Gold Crown*, also named after the saint, dating from the time of Charles IV (according to legend, it is quite dangerous as it is reputed to cause the death of anyone who wears it without any right, within a year), the *sceptre* and the *imperial pommel* from the time of Ferdinand I.

PRAGUE CASTLE

ST. JOANNES BAPT.

S. WENCESLAUS. S. WOLFGANG. S. JOANNA.

Wenceslaus
Sigismund
Moramet3
cum uxorem
Joanna nata
Küfer
ab Assmansvilla
1875.

Cathedral of St Vitus

CHAPEL OF ST WENCESLAS

The Chapel has a square plan, is larger in size than the other chapels and is also more sophisticated with almost 1,350 semi-precious stones set into the walls creating a grandiose frame for the fresco cycle dedicated to the *Passion of Christ* (1372-1373). This chapel is, moreover, the most sacred as it houses the relics of prince Wenceslas, patron saint of Bohemia, on the same spot where they were originally buried, in what was then the St Vitus rotunda.

A fine door (above) leads to the stairway up to the Crown Room. Higher up, the chapel has a second fresco cycle, dated 16th-17th century and representing scenes from the life of St Wenceslas. The chapel also contains an unusual tower-shaped reliquary (on the left) and an excellent painted stone statue of the saint (1373), probably by a nephew of Petr Parléř, (below) standing against the background of another fresco with angels and saints.

The Royal Palace

From the Royal Oratory of the Cathedral a covered passage leads directly to the old Royal Palace, on the south side of the Third Courtyard. The building came into being in the 12th century when prince Soběslav I had the first royal residence built here in Romanesque style and with a rectangular plan.

Above, the exterior of the Vladislav Hall, the stronghold of the old Royal Palace; below, the ancient passage linking the Cathedral to the Royal Palace.
Right, view of the Third Courtyard, with the statue of St George facing the entrance to the Royal Palace.

The massive south walls of the palace also became part of the Castle defences. In 1185 the Chapel of All Saints was constructed alongside and in the middle of the 13th century, Přemysl Otakar II had the palace enlarged. It was not until the 14th century when Charles IV was still only the hereditary prince, that the building was significantly enlarged towards the north and the west, thus acquiring space to create the large reception rooms, and the Gothic style was supplanted by the Romanesque. When Wenceslas IV in turn decided that rebuilding was required, he intended to transform the palace into a comfortable and elegant residence for the royal family, though he also extended the buildings and modified the direct passage between the palace and Chapel of All Saints. Due to the Hussite wars the palace was for long abandoned and it was king Vladislav Jagellonsky who restored it to its regal function and status, financing a series of impressive building projects involving in particular the first floor and especially the creation of the attractive Vladislav Hall. After the disastrous fire of 1541 it was Ferdinand I of Hapsburg who had to tackle the problem of the serious damage caused, at the same time rebuilding the Hall of the Diets. As time passed, however, the palace gradually ceased to be used for its original function, first losing its role as a residence for the royal family (the Hapsburgs in fact preferred the rooms in the western part of the castle) while the administrative function was greatly reduced, though it continued to fulfil a role as the setting for important public ceremonies. Lastly, as part of the project for radically rebuilding the entire castle carried out in the 18th century by Nicola Pacassi and commissioned by Empress Maria Theresa, the façades were all modified to achieve an appearance in complete harmony with the surrounding buildings and the old Royal Palace was thus definitively integrated with the new Hapsburg image of this imposing complex.

THE INTERIOR

Preceded by the graceful *Eagle Fountain* (1664, made by Francesco Torre), access to the old Royal Palace is through a resplendent 18th century façade and the effect is not unlike travelling back through history. In many of the rooms, halls and stairways it feels almost as though time has stood still. First is the **Green Room**, where at first Charles IV supervised the discussion of minor legal problems and later a fully fledged court tribunal was established at the beginning of the 16th century. Nearby is the first majestic example of the rebuilding carried out by Vladislav Jagellonsky – the huge and spectacular **Vladislav Hall**, commissioned from Benedikt Ried by Vladislav Jagellonsky and replacing three earlier Gothic rooms (in-

cluding the Throne Room) dating from the time of Charles IV. Some 62 metres long, 16 metres wide and 13 metres high, built between 1492 and 1502 it was the largest room in Europe at the time – large enough indeed to house, as well as the usual ceremonies, equestrian tournaments and even a market. The Hall was greatly admired, especially for the extraordinary design of the groins and the highly elegant 'star-shaped' curved vault and the excellent light provided by the large windows clearly of early Renaissance inspiration. The entire structure is in fact pervaded by a sensation of daring architectural innovation which, departing from late Gothic principles, clearly heralded the new refinements brought by the Renaissance. Lit

by five large antique chandeliers made of tin (16th century), the president of the Republic was elected in this room. From here there is a splendid view over the gardens to the south and, built by Vladislav Jagellonsky for his son Ludvík, the Renaissance south wing (also known as the **Ludvík Wing**) with a splendid panoramic balcony, is reached. Located here are the two **Halls of the Chancellery of Bohemia**, where the supreme institutional organ after the sovereign met. The first was the officials' room and has an elegant late Gothic vault decorated with a web of ribbing, while the second is noted for having been the setting for the episode known as the Prague Defenestration.
Many other rooms in the Royal

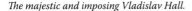

The majestic and imposing Vladislav Hall.

The Hall of the Diet, with the solemn royal throne and 19th-century furnishings.

THE EQUESTRIAN STAIR

Indirect confirmation that rousing equestrian tournaments took place in the Vladislav Hall is provided by the existence of the original Equestrian Stairway, located where the entrance to the earlier Throne Room of Charles IV was, and entered from St George's Square. It was specifically built to provide a suitable entrance for the horses as is clearly obvious from the original steps which are smooth and so low as to be little more than a gentle hump. The knights were therefore able to pay homage to the king in a dignified manner without having to descend from their horses to climb the stairs.

king, seated on the throne and with the archbishop of Prague at his side, promulgated the governmental provisions that drastically reduced the privileges and rights of the rebellious Czech States. Splendidly presented in this room are the *tribune* used by the clerks and the large *portraits* of the principal members of the imperial family – Maria Theresa and her husband, Franz of Lorraine, Joseph II, Leopold II and Francis II. Further north, on the ground floor, at the point of the Equestrian Stair, is the surviving part of the Gothic wing. This formed part of the palace of Charles IV, with the Office of the **Old Land Registry**, probably dating from the time of Oldrich II and damaged by the 1541 fire which also destroyed most of

Left, one of the four rooms of the New Land Property Registry, showing the coats of arms of all those who worked there between 1561 and 1774. Below, the first room of the Chancellery of Bohemia, with an elegant 17th-century majolica stove.

Palace are worthy of note: the brightly-lit Renaissance **Council Room of the Imperial Court**, where in 1621 the sentence of death by beheading of the nobles who had taken part in the rebellion against the Hapsburgs was publicly announced; the four rooms of the 16th-century **New Land Property Registry** connected to the Vladislav Hall by an attractive spiral stairway; the **Room of the Diet** on the north east of the Vladslav Hall. This is situated in the wing built by Wenceslas IV and restructured by Vladislav Jagellonsky, destroyed by the fire of 1541 and rebuilt by the architect Wohlmut, who chose to replace the ribs so characteristic of Gothic vaults, though purely as a decorative element. Seat of the supreme tribunal and of the assembly of the Czech States, this room is now furnished with 19th-century pieces though they reproduce the appearance of some two centuries earlier when, in 1627 the

the archives with incalculable losses; the arcaded **courtyard** dating from the time of Charles IV, though some arches were bricked up by his son Wenceslas. Also here are the 14th-century **Gothic Hall** under the floor of which an even older Romanesque room has been discovered, and the **Hall of Charles IV**, created by joining together three separate rooms, while Charles' son Wenceslas IV was responsible for the curved vaulting. This room now houses interesting models that illustrate the historical and architectural evolution of the old Royal Palace. Lastly is the elegant **Wenceslas IV Hall of Columns,** named for the two columns that support the vault. Following the subsequent phases of building, the older Romanesque complex has now receded to the state and position of underground rooms (and in the course of centuries they have also been used as cellars). However, still surviving beside the remains of some ancient fortifications are interesting traces of the old *south gate* and a large *hall* with barrel vaulting, almost 50 metres long, providing access to the crypt of the neighbouring Chapel of All Saints.

CHAPEL OF ALL SAINTS

Through a Renaissance doorway made by Giovanni Gargiolli in the Hall of Vladislav, the sovereigns of Bohemia could directly reach the balcony of the neighbouring All Saints Chapel commissioned by Charles IV and built in Gothic style between 1370 and 1387 by Petr Parléř taking the Sainte Chapelle in Paris as his model. A Romanesque Chapel of the Princes (1185) already stood on this spot. But the church we see today, crowned with a Renaissance vault and embellished with a baroque high altar, is the result of substantial late 16th century rebuilding made necessary by the damage caused by the fire of 1541. The rebuilding had an exceptional patron in Elisabeth, queen of France who was the widow of Charles IX and sister of Rudolph II. Since 1588 the remains of St Procopius, a patron saint of Bohemia, have been housed in this church.

A view of the interior of the austere Chapel of All Saints.

St George's Monastery and Basilica

St George's was originally the main square in the Castle and, before the building of the Cathedral, was much larger than today. Prince Vratislav I had a single nave church built here in 920, consecrated in 925 and destined to house the remains of the first Czech martyr, his mother princess Ludmilla, who was canonised shortly after and was also the grandmother of another, future saint, Wenceslas the son of Vratislav. In 973 Boleslaus II and his sister, the abbess Mlada, built the neighbouring monastery and it consequently became necessary to enlarge this little church transforming it into a basilica with three naves, three apses to the east and two crypts. In the years to come the Přemyslid sovereigns were to be buried here, signifying the importance this religious building had now acquired. Seriously damaged during the siege of 1142, the church was rebuilt quite a bit longer, and with two **towers**, the more northerly one of which would be integrated into the cloister during the baroque period, while the more southerly one was probably built on the spot where the Chapel of the Virgin Mary had stood in the past, probably over the site of the original burial place of St Ludmilla. The **chapel** built to house the remains of the saint dates from the 13th century and is located on the

Top, the façade of the Chapel of St George.
Above, a detail of one of the two symmetrical baroque stairways which lead from the funerary monuments of the Přemyslid princes to the square choir.

south side of the Romanesque apse (the stone *sepulchre* is instead a 14th-century work by Petr Parléř, commissioned by Charles IV). A new *west façade* was made during the 14th century, also by Petr Parléř. It was remodelled with red brickwork in baroque style in the 17th century and in the same century the **Chapel of St John Nepomucene** was made in the south west corner of the basilica and decorated with a stupendous baroque *fresco* in the cupola representing the *Apotheosis of St John Nepomucene*, by Václav Reiner. The *south façade* is also interesting with a Romanesque wall that encloses a Renaissance doorway leading to the south nave and dated 1515, a magnificent creation by Benedikt Ried.

Originally entrusted to the Benedictine nuns for the education of young daughters of the Bohemian aristocracy, the evolution of the monastery was similar to that of the church. It was also badly damaged during the siege of 1142 but was quickly rebuilt larger and with an additional storey. Helped by the fact that its abbesses usually belonged to aristocratic families, if not indeed the royal family, the convent quickly grew in size and importance, with the addition of a large Gothic cloister, while the abbesses acquired the right and privilege of crowning the queen of Bohemia. Destroyed by the fire of 1541, rebuilt in Renaissance style, completely restructured a century later according to the new dictates of the baroque style, including an entirely new **cloister** which replaced the older Gothic one altogether, this powerful monastery was suppressed in 1782 by Joseph II and the building was transformed into a barracks. Despite the baroque façade, the interior of the church still has an austere Romanesque appearance with lofty women's

Above, a general view of the nave. Left, one of the chapels in the basilica and, below, the frescoes that enhance the dome of the baroque chapel of St John Nepomucene.

galleries, *funerary monuments* marking the sepulchres of the Přemyslid princes, including the sepulchre of the church's founder, Vratislav I, fine *frescoes* in the conches of the apses and chapels, and a *crypt* with 12th-century cross vaults. Since 1975, on the first floor the monastery has housed the **section of the National Gallery in Prague** dedicated to the Mannerist paintings belonging to the court of Rudolph II as well as Bohemian baroque works of the 17th and 18th centuries, with works of art by H. Von Aachen, Spranger, A. De Vries, P. Brandl, V. V. Reiner and M. B. Braun.

Peter Johannes Brandl, Apostle, *1725*

Jan Kupecky, Portrait of the miniaturist, Karl Bruni, *1709*

Matyas Bernard Braun, Saint Lutgard by the Cross, *1710*

Adrian de Vries, Bronze horse, *1610*

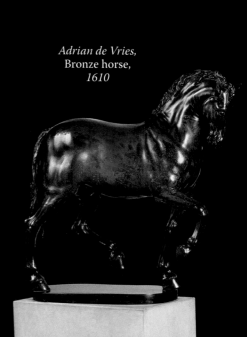

PRAGUE CASTLE

Golden Lane

Running in a west to east direction behind St George's Monastery, this picturesque and romantic little street, also known as Alchemists' Lane, is an obligatory port of call for visitors to the Castle and represents the tradition of Prague as a "magical city". In dark and smoky laboratories here Rudolph II's alchemists sought to reveal the myths of the philosopher's stone and the production of gold. The tale is one of the most intriguing to have developed about the city and its Castle. The reality is that the Renaissance houses along this lane were built in the second half of the 16th century to replace twenty or so temporary and ramshackle houses that had sprung up here set against the Castle walls, incorporating the remains of the medieval fortifications to the south and replac-

ing the older defensive terraces to the north, in order to provide lodgings for Rudolph II's servants and guards. It was later that the goldsmiths also moved into this area. Many centuries later, between 1916 and 1917, at number 22 of the Lane, Franz Kafka wrote some of his short stories. Today the little houses that once were craftsmen's workshops and dwellings for the poor, are attractive shops where souvenirs and artistic and crafts items can be bought. A quite delightful view can be enjoyed from the castle walls behind, where a long *defensive corridor* winds its way along the top of the houses, still providing a connection between the late Gothic terraces of the fortifications and the Castle itself.

Views of the colourful and picturesque cottages in the Golden Lane.

Lobkovicz Palace

Opposite the Burgrave's House stands an impressive building structured around two courtyards. The Lobokovicz Palace was the residence of the powerful Pernštejn family during the 16th century and in 1627 after being extended, it passed to the owners for whom it is now named. Between 1651 and 1668 the Lobkovicz family had the buildings entirely restructured by Carlo Lurago in baroque style. Some of the rooms on the first floor, such as the two halls and nearby chapel, are still in their original state, while the rest of the palace houses the **section of the National Museum** dedicated to the ancient history of Bohemia.

One of the splendid interiors of Lobkovicz Palace.

Black Tower

Closing the Castle and its fortifications on the west are a gate and tower, both interesting remains of what were the Romanesque walls dating from the mid-12th century. The Black Tower was originally known as the Golden Tower after the polished gilding of the roof that glistened at the time of Charles IV, but it was a victim of the 1541 fire which definitively destroyed the gilding and gave rise to its current name. However, the Black Tower was part of the Burgrave's buildings and was for long used as the prison where condemned debtors were held. The Renaissance style *East Door* still has the low Gothic passageway as well as the pulleys used to raise the drawbridge which crossed the moat in front. Where this moat once was there is now a small panoramic square with access to the *Old Castle Stairway*, leading down towards the city.

Above, the eastern gate of Prague Castle beneath the sombre Black Tower. Right, the Old Castle Stairway, a romantic and almost legendary part of Prague, celebrated in popular songs, which leads down into the city from the East Gate.

SOUTH GARDENS

The **South Gardens** on the southern side of the Castle are quite delightful; they are connected to the Third Courtyard by the *Bull Staircase* and consist of the **Garden on the Ramparts** (*Zahrada Na Valech*) and the **Paradise Garden** (*Rajska Zahrada*) which were already well developed in the 16th century, but redesigned and improved during the 20th century by Plečnik. In the shade of the dramatic and majestic south façade of the Castle, skilfully rearranged by Pacassi, the gardens are a series of incredible botanical features, historical ruins and artistic masterpieces.

Castle Gardens

Once the Castle no longer needed to fulfil a function as a purely defensive stronghold, and it had become possible to emphasize its role as a noble residence used for purposes of representation, it was finally possible to develop its more pleasant and enjoyable aspects. Thus, around the perimeter of the fortifications delightful gardens came into being and thrived. It was the Hapsburg sovereign, Ferdinand I, who oversaw their creation in 1534, but their present splendid appearance, enhanced by the presence of numerous Renaissance and baroque statues, is thanks to the 20th-century architect Josip Plečnik who began their reorganization after 1918, an arduous task that is not entirely completed even today.

Bust of Josip Plečnik in the South Gardens.

The **Bellevue Pavilion** was made by Plečnik in 1924 with faintly Egyptian overtones and a splendid viewpoint. There is also an **Alpine Flower Garden**, the **Hartig Garden**, which only became part of the South Gardens in 1965, the **Matthias Pavilion**, a cylindrical structure made in 1617 for Emperor Matthias, as well as two little stone monu-

THE PRAGUE DEFENESTRATION

Historically two defenestrations took place in Prague: the first was in 1419 and was a prelude to the Hussite War, and the second – the only really famous one – took place on 23 May 1618. At the time the lieutenant who was deputizing for the sovereign and governing the country in his absence, was installed in the second Room of the Chancellery and here on that fateful day in May the aristocratic representatives of the strongly Protestant Czech states came to express their discontent at the election of Ferdinand II of Hapsburg, a Catholic and clearly more sympathetic to that religion, as Emperor of the Holy Roman Empire and consequently also sovereign of Bohemia. Their protest took the form of a rather implausible trial which ended with the lieutenant, another governor belonging to the pro-Austrian part, and the clerk present at the meeting all being thrown out of the window. Although they fell from quite a height, they ended up on a pile of dung that broke their fall, saving their lives and limiting the gravity of the consequences. The event had more serious results on the historical level, as this defenestration lead first of all to the rebellion of the Czech states and then to the Thirty Years War.

*Above and right, two views of the
Paradise Garden (Rajska Zahrada)
and the unmistakable decorative granite bowl.
Below, statues flanking the Musical Pavilion
in the Hartig Garden.*

*Facing page, above, the Noblewomen's Institute
seen from the Garden on the Ramparts
(Zahrada Na Valech).*

ments close by the Ludvík Wing commemorating the spot where two of the unfortunate victims of the Prague Defenestration fell. Seen from this elegant green paradise, even the Castle seems to assume a sweeter and softer appearance. And from here we return to the Castle, to the west entrance standing at the end of the route through the South Gardens.

Charming views of the elegant gardens to the north of the Castle: above, and top facing page, the Summer Palace of Queen Anne, with the 16th-century Singing Fountain in front; below, the balustrade and fountain near the old president's residence and a detail of one of the 18th-century statues, portraying children playing with the lions.

ROYAL GARDENS

Along the fortifications on the north is the crevice of a deep gulley with a stream which, once its obvious use as a defensive feature became superfluous, fell into disuse and was been substantially abandoned, evolving into a pleasant shelter for many animals, including deer. There are no longer any deer, but their presence in the past is still clearly evoked by the name of the **Deer Moat**. The **Powder Bridge** crosses it in the area of the old 17th-century **Stables** and **Riding School** as well as the famous **Lions' Court**. At the back of this courtyard lie the splendid **Royal Gardens**, for centuries famous for their tropical plants, the exotic fruits that could be gathered there, and the fertile vegetable gardens. Moreover, it was here that certain bulbs imported from Istanbul were cultivated and the tulips that bloomed were then imported by Holland. It was precisely to provide easier access to this magnificent corner of the gardens that the Powder Bridge was built in the mid 16th century. The pretty pathways are enhanced by various elegant buildings, such as the large **Real Tennis Pavilion** (the oldest stone building of its kind in Europe, it was built in 1569 by Wohlmut) and the **Orangery**, originally 16th century, but attractively renovated in the 20th century. Also known as the Belvedere for its wonderful view, the **Summer Palace of Queen Anne** is at the end, beyond the small garden; built by Ferdinand I for his wife, Anne Jagellonsky between 1535 and 1563, it has an unusual roof shaped like the keel of a boat and is surrounded by delightful airy arches. It is difficult to imagine that this pretty, delicate building was destined to be used as a barracks and army workshop for almost a century between the 1700s and 1800s.

Right, a detail of the Real Tennis Pavilion, enhanced with statues; below, the Cathedral seen from the Riding School gardens.

PALÁCOVÉ GARDENS

One of the most recent developments within the area of the gardens that lie to the south of the Castle, below what used to be a powerful system of defensive ramparts, involves the group of gardens collectively known as the **Palácové Zahrady**, "Palace Gardens". In the 16th century pre-existing parklands and vineyards were transformed into splendid Italianate gardens and a century later, following their destruction by the occupying Swedish, the owners of the palaces overlooking the area had a new baroque layout created, decorated with many statues, balustrades, terraces and fountains. In the late 20th century a sweeping initiative brought about the complete restoration of the old structures and has lead to the rebirth of five of the old gardens: *Ledeburská, Malá Pálffyovská, Velká Pálffyovská, Kolowratská,* and *Malá Fürstenberská.* The first two were opened to the public in June 1995, the third in 1997 and the last two in 2000. Admired and supported by the European Union, the initiative has restored one of its most delightful features to the city of Prague.

Delightful views of the Palácové Gardens,
recently restored to their original splendour.

CONTENTS